OCEANS

Life Beneath The Waves

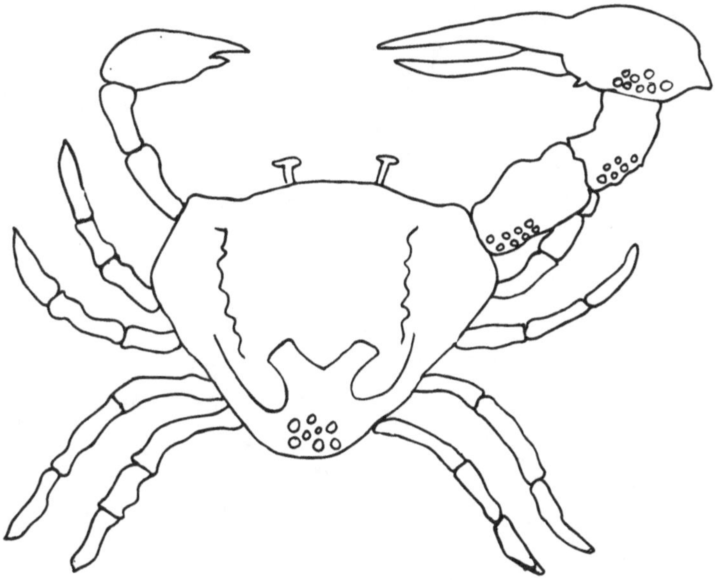

Illustrated by
Raina Van Luchene

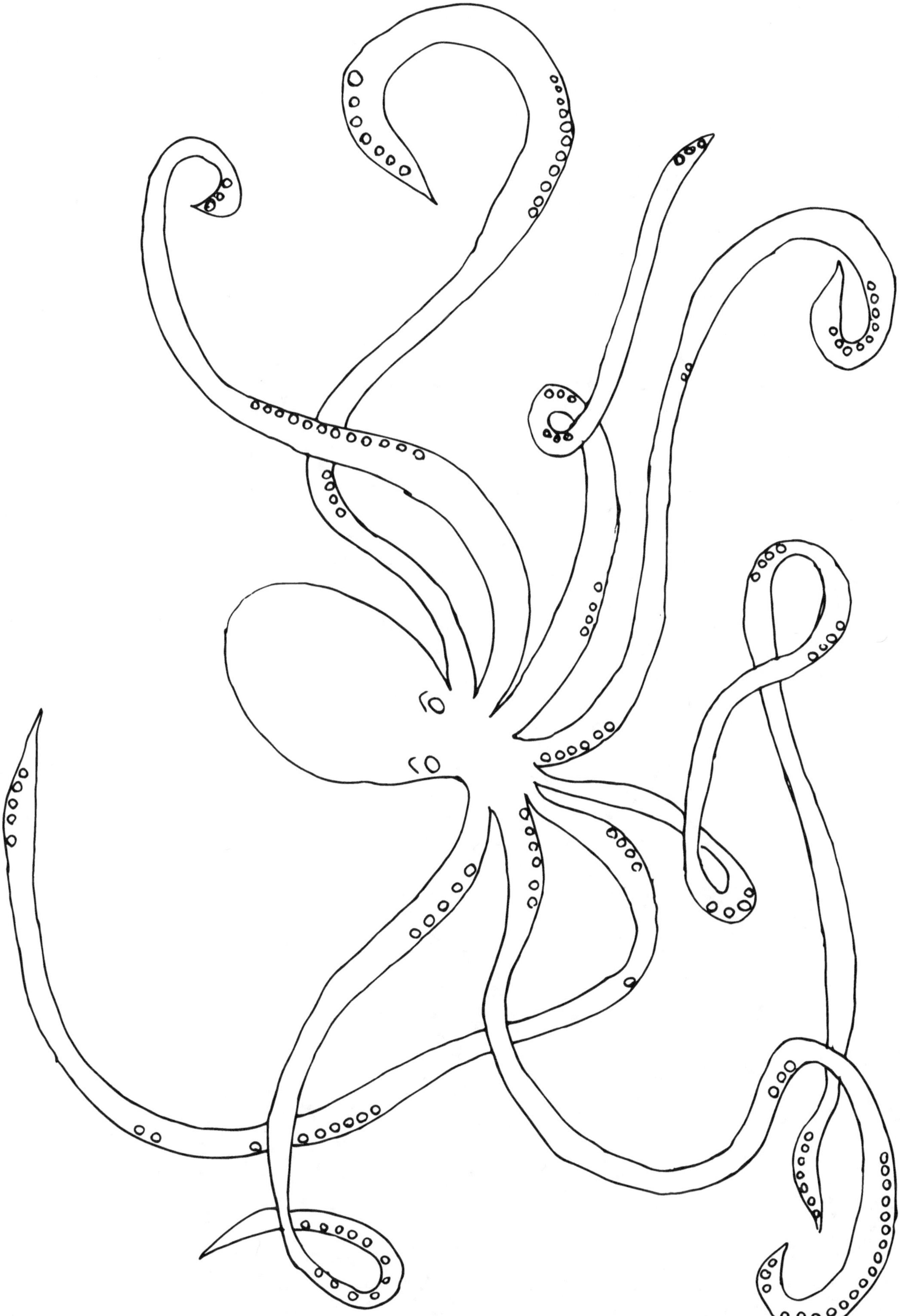

A

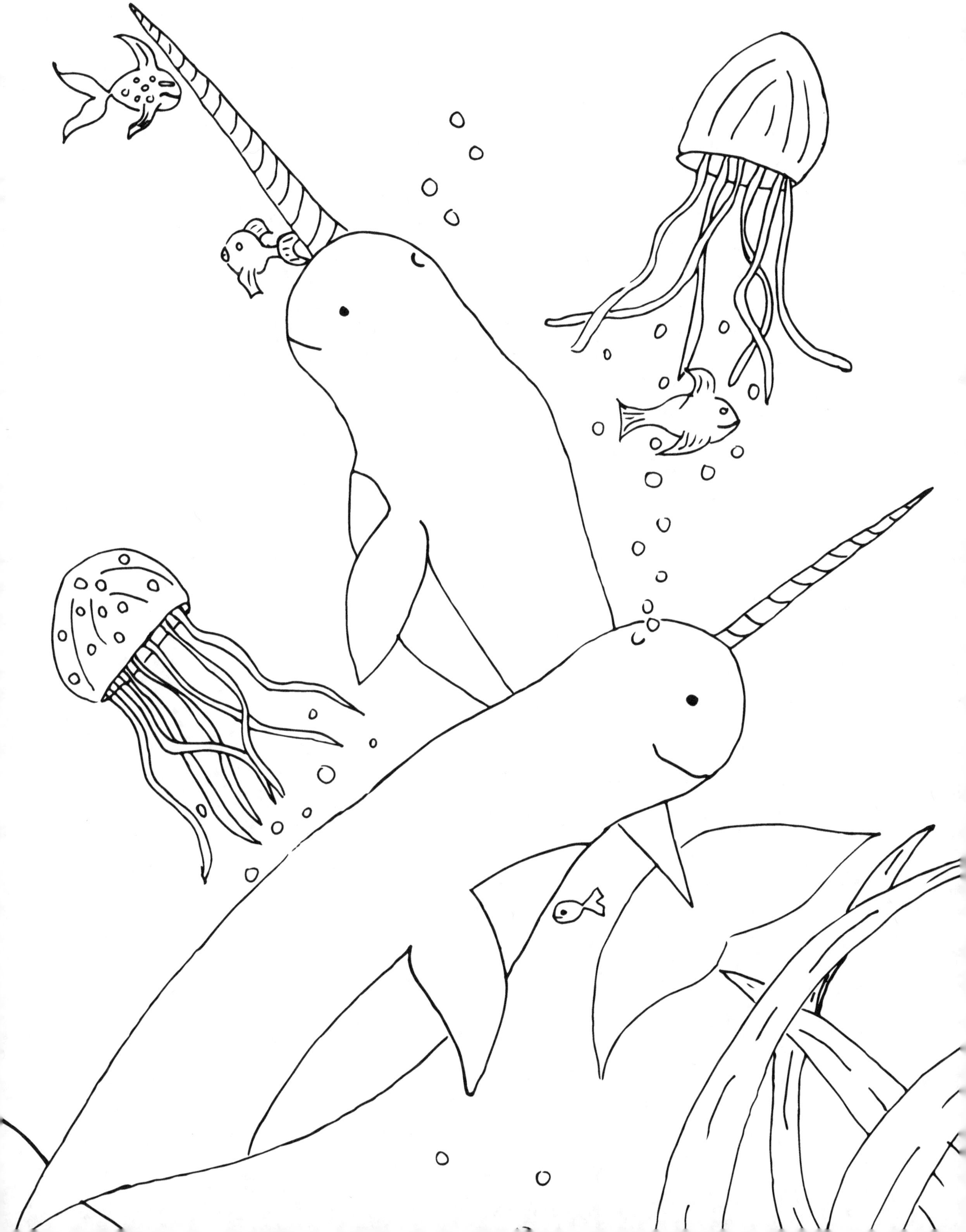

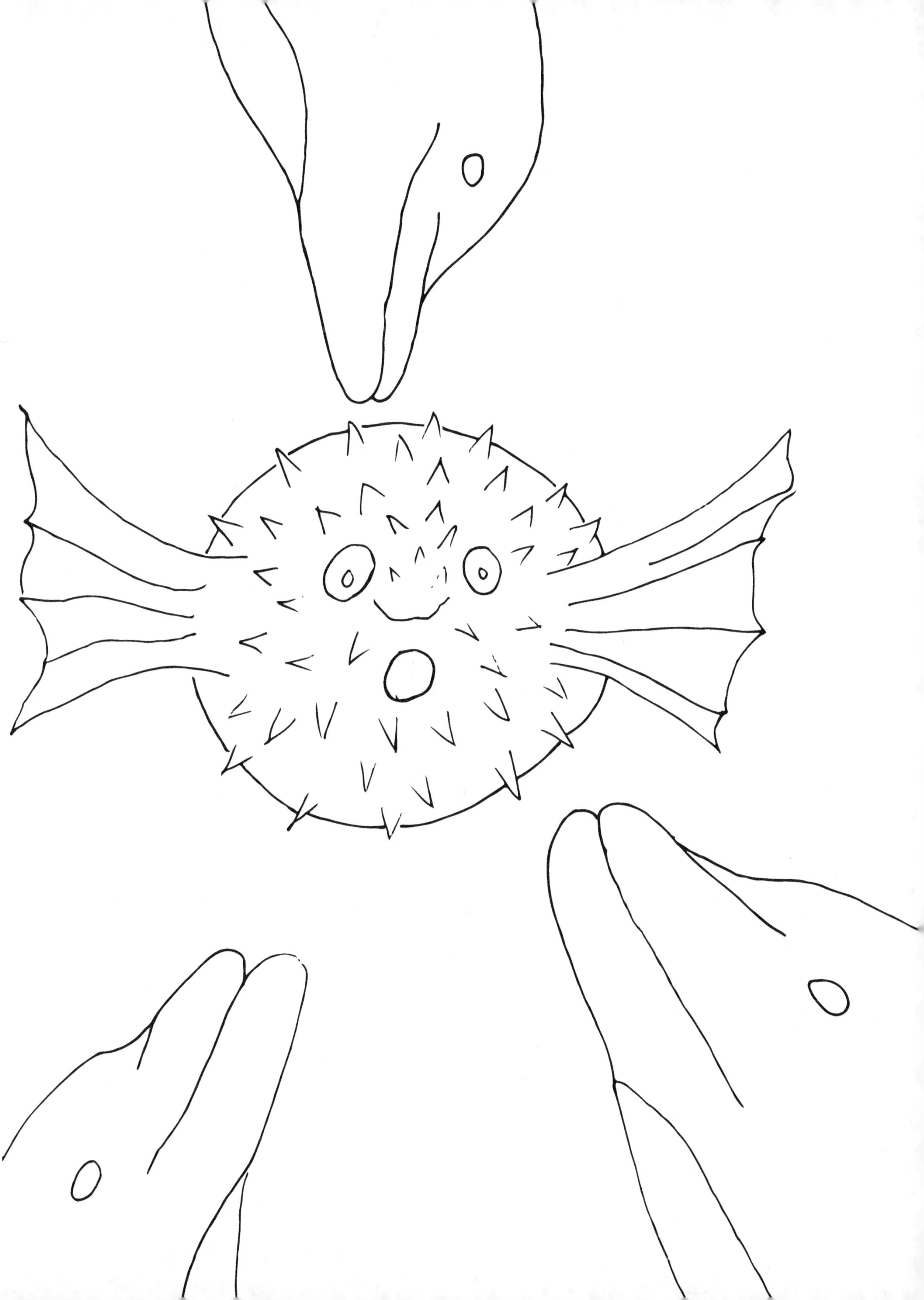

I just want HUGS

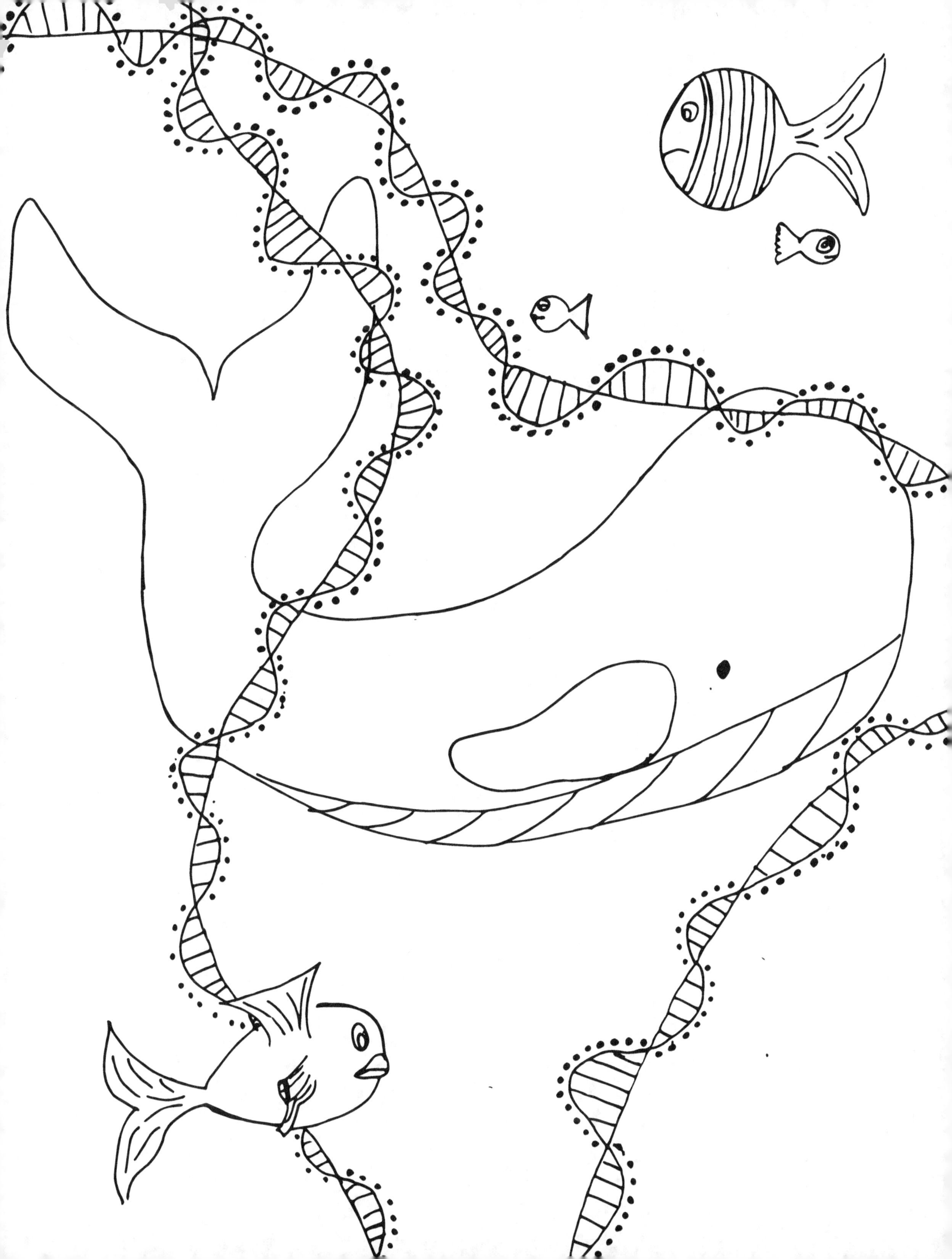

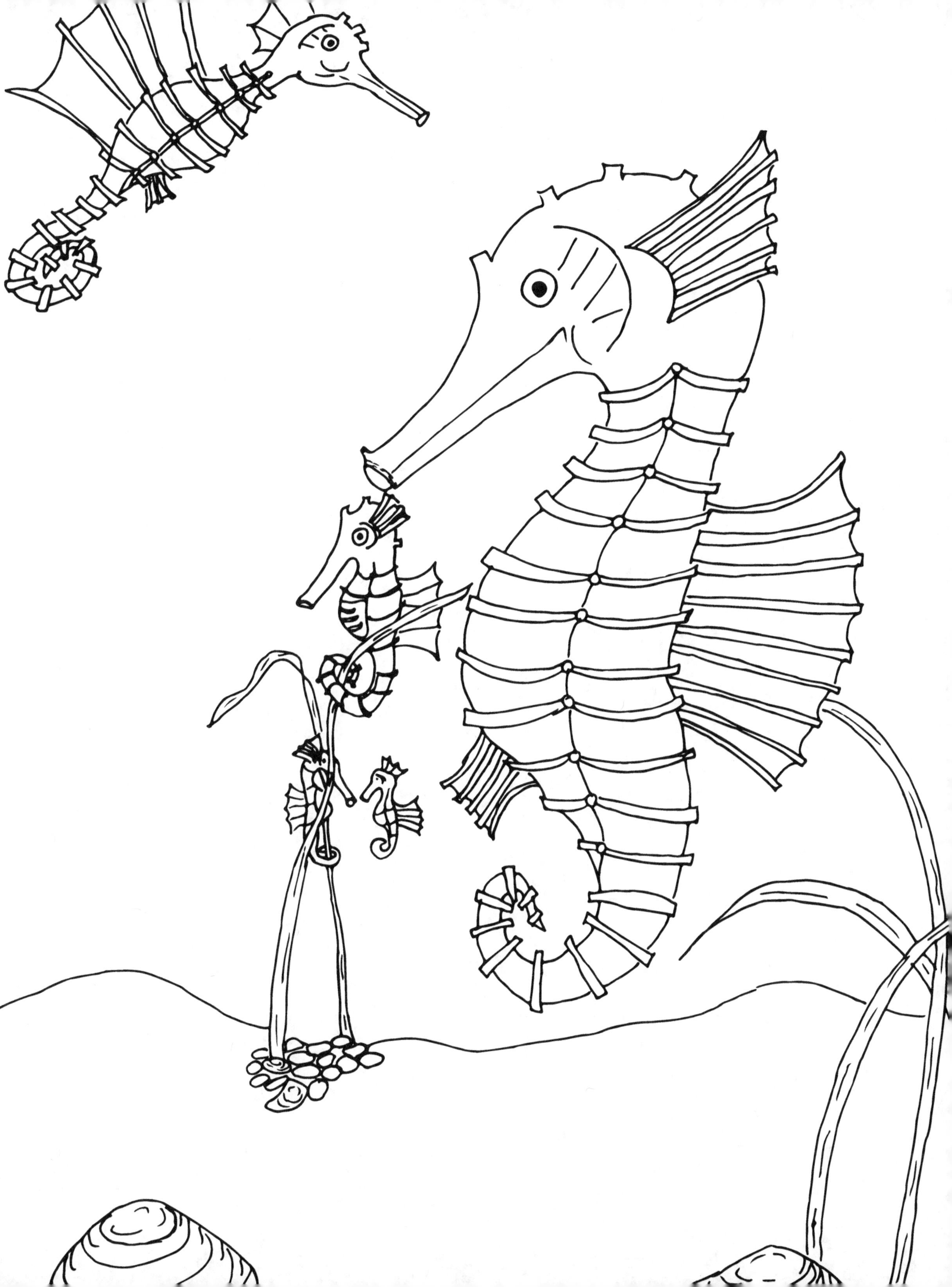

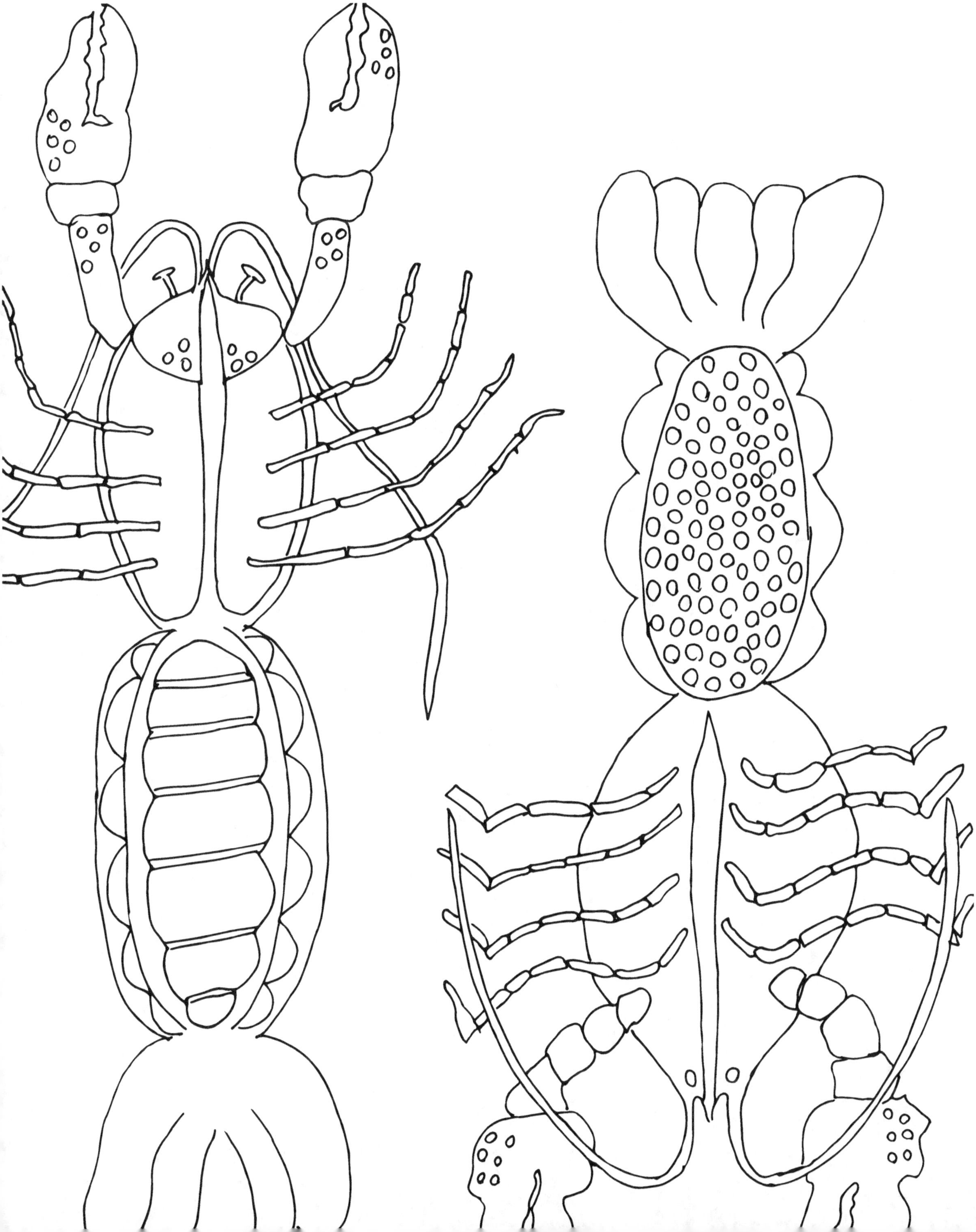

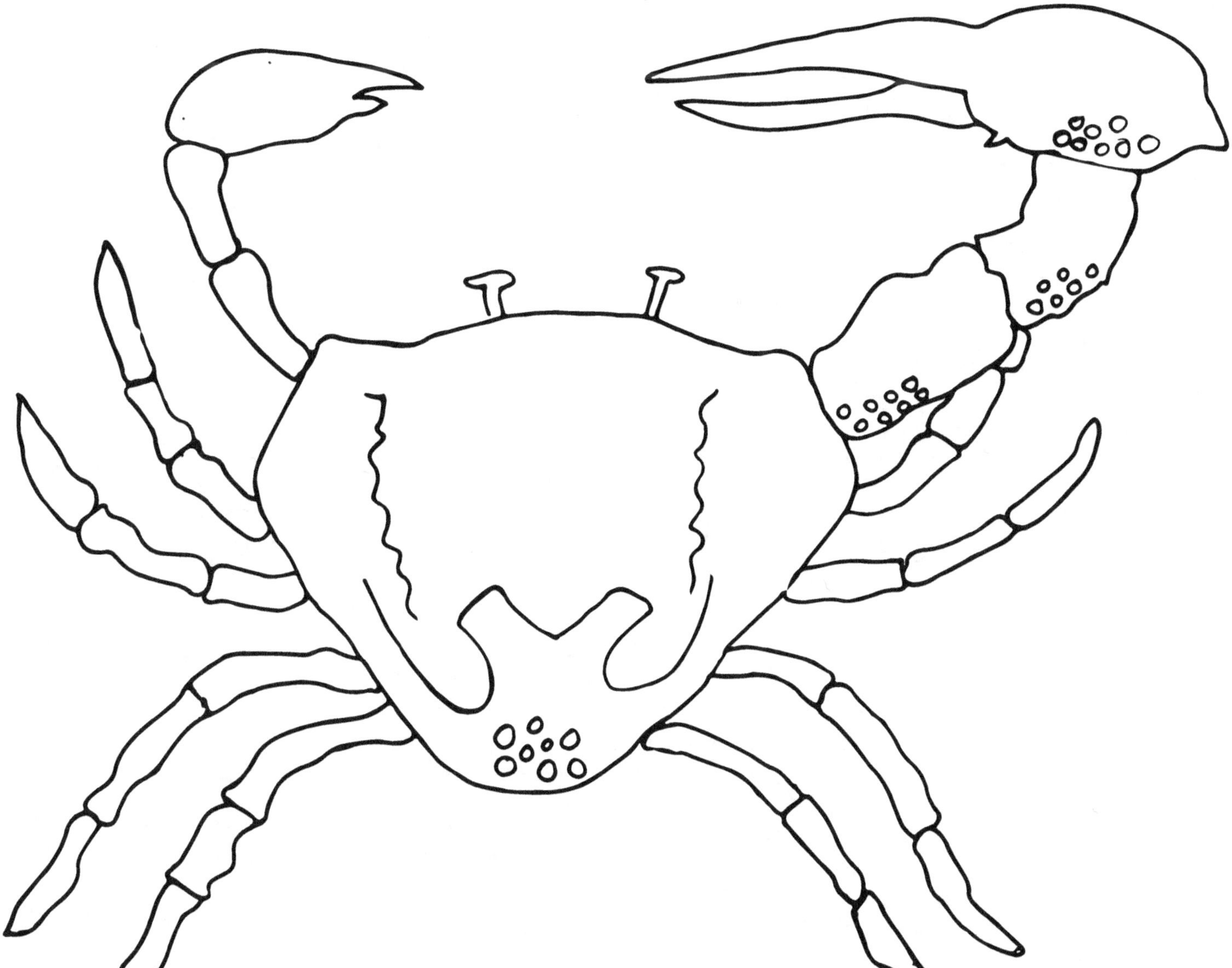

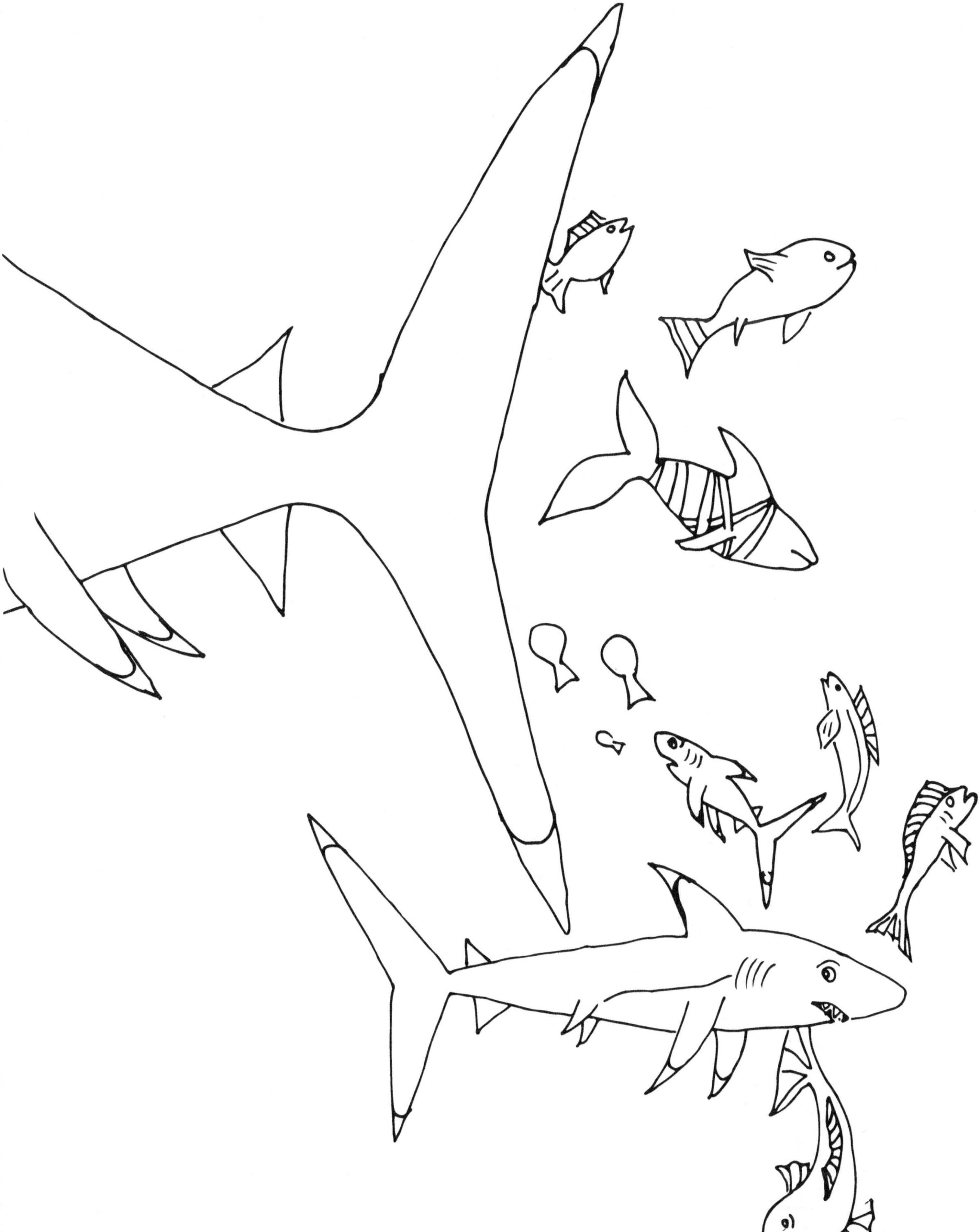

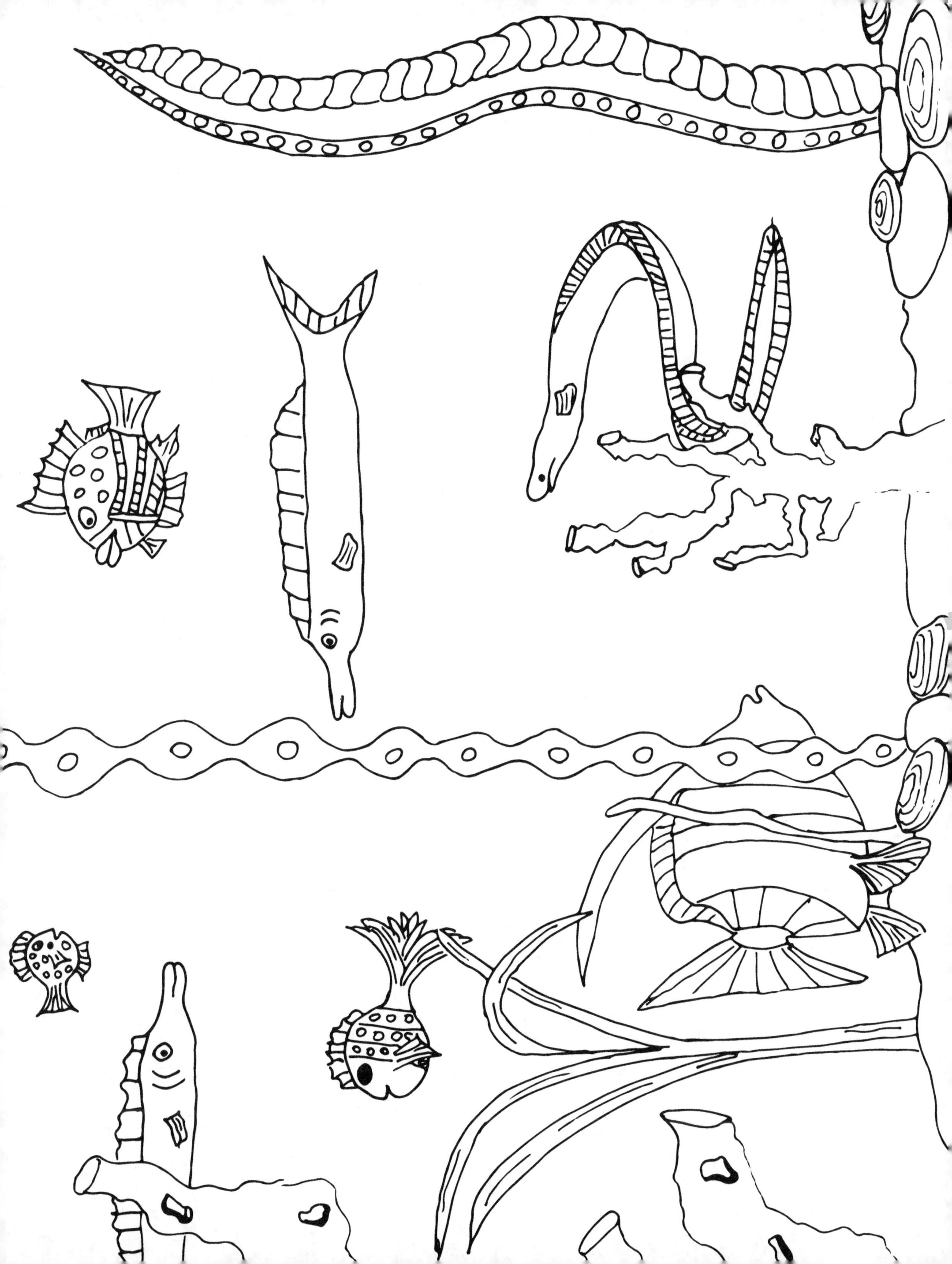

Not all stars...
... belong to the Sky.

www.ingramcontent.com/pod-product-compliance
Lightning Source LLC
Chambersburg PA
CBHW081153280526
45787CB00008B/3311
* 9 7 8 1 5 3 4 7 2 4 2 8 0 *